To Janet

Best wishes

Jackie Huck

Cats Like Me

By Jackie Huck

Illustrations by Pauline Henderson

2QT Limited (Publishing)

This First Edition published 2010
2QT Limited (Publishing)
Dalton Lane, Burton In Kendal
Cumbria LA6 1NJ
www.2qt.co.uk

Artwork by Pauline Henderson
Printed in Great Britain by
the MPG Books Group, Bodmin and King's Lynn

Mixed Sources

Product group from well-managed
forests, controlled sources and
recycled wood or fiber
www.fsc.org Cert no. TT-COC-002303
© 1996 Forest Stewardship Council

FSC

A CIP catalogue record for this book is available
from the British Library
ISBN 978-1-908098-12-2

Contents

This book is dedicated to
cat lovers everywhere,
and to the many precious cats
who have enriched my life

THE SULTAN

I'm not the only cat in the house
more's the pity I fear,
I never make trouble,
or dirty my paws,
No sound of complaint do they hear;
But - There's never a word for
The Sultan,

As I sit here quiet and tall,
They pass me by
with never a glance,
As if I were part of the wall.
The others, are stroked
as they sit by the fire,
They have sardines
and kippers for tea,
They create such a fuss,
they scatter their hairs,
Not one of them's better than me;
But - There's never a word for
The Sultan,

As I sit here all alone,
They never even think of me,
I could be made of stone.
The others, those lazy, fat felines,
Asleep on my Mistress's knee,
They wake just to eat,
and they never say "thanks",
There's none of them
purr - fect, like me,
But - There's never a word for
The Sultan,

As I sit here by myself,
If only some day,
some kind soul would say,
"What a nice China Cat, on that shelf."

THE TALE OF

TIMOTHY TRAVELLER

Timothy arrived one bitter winter evening back in the 1980's. The wind was blowing the first flakes of a heavy snowfall against the windows, and as I popped out of the back door to put out the rubbish this large grey and white cat slipped between my legs.

He wandered around the hall sniffing. Satisfied, he headed for the living room. A few minutes later he was warming himself against the Rayburn, oblivious to the disgruntled hissing from the other cats.

I offered a plate of food which was accepted with grace and eaten in seconds to the dregs. A second plateful disappeared more slowly, followed by a big bowl of milk. He lingered for a few more minutes, enjoying a quiet wash. This done, he headed back to the door and asked to be let out. Off into the blizzard he went, and I truly wondered if I would see him again.

He was waiting the next morning, and walked in as the previous night. Thoroughly at home, he pushed his way through the cat family, and before I knew was helping himself to their breakfast. Amazingly, apart from a few slight hisses (which he ignored) they accepted him. Breakfast eaten he looked around the room, discovered the cat basket, curled up, and within a few minutes was asleep.

So his routine became established. After food he slept until evening. He woke about seven, washed and enjoyed a good supper, then went out for the night, but was always waiting in the morning. He enjoyed attention, but was reserved in giving affection. He did not make friends of the other cats, but tolerated them, accepting it was their home he was sharing. I never heard him growl, but his purr was loud.

Christmas came and went, and we headed into the New Year. January and February slipped away, March passed and April brought the herald of spring, with a gradual warming.

We'd become accustomed to Timothy by now, and looked forward to seeing him each morning, and tried not to disturb his slumbers during the day.

It was about the second week in April, the daffodils were stirring, all was in bud. Timothy came in as usual, ate a good breakfast and slept until evening. He woke at his normal time, devoured an extra large plate of food, and asked for extra milk.

Then, instead of heading for the door, he went round all the cats. They had also grown used to him, and accepted his rubbing round their heads, although it was not his normal habit to push his attentions on them.

His rounds of the cat family finished he then turned his attention to the humans. He went from one to the other, tangling around our legs, meowing, purring, asking to be stroked and nursed. Never had Timothy been so affectionate. This display of love went on for about half an hour. At last he seemed satisfied, and headed for the door.

It was a lovely, warm spring evening. A gentle breeze stirred Timothy's fur as he walked out. For a few seconds he lingered, looking back. Then as on so many evenings before, he was gone, but this time it was different, and I never saw him again.

He wasn't there next morning, and in a strange way I wasn't surprised. He'd said his 'Goodbye's' the evening before, I believe he also said 'Thank you' for a winter of warmth, comfort and love. As suddenly as he came into our lives, he left. I missed him dreadfully, and for weeks looked for him every morning, but it wasn't to be.

I had the feeling he was in transit. Going somewhere, hopefully to some home he'd left. He had broken his journey with us, and stayed a winter, but now his purpose returned, and he had to carry on. I often think of him, and hope he reached his 'home', wherever it was.

HOW ALBERT RABBIT

LOST HIS EARS

I know he had 'em when he left,
         he wasn't long away,
But he came back without 'em,
         it fairly spoilt 'me day.
I was nibbling on some clover
         when this sorry sound I hears,
And there stood Albert Rabbit
         back without his ears!

He said he'd had a mishap
         down where the brambles grow,
Where nosey Albert Rabbit went
         where rabbits oughtn't go,
For as he pried and poked about
         in between a tasty munch,
He came upon Black Tom the cat
         sleeping off his lunch.

Before Albert had the time to flee
               Black Tom leapt with delight,
And dug his teeth in Albert,
                    and held on very tight.
He lugged Albert round the garden
               sort of showing off his prize,
And Albert saw his little life,
                    flash before his eyes.

Then with much sniggering and growling,
          (Oh! The thought quite makes me ill)
Tom started chewing Albert,
                without even makin't kill,
And all't poor chap could find to do
           was to lie there dead and dumb,
Whilst' cat chomped through
                        our Albert's ears
He ate 'em, one by one!

Some say it was a miracle,
                others just good luck,
For no rabbit's lived to tell the tale
                when Tom the cat has struck,
But as Albert lay there faking death
                in between those massive paws,
He heard a yawn and then a purr
                then deep contented snores.

It was the only chance that Albert had,
                he didn't wait to think,
Up he sprang and scampered off
                and was gone within a blink.
Across the garden, through the fence
          past the brambles where he'd dined,
As fast as his feet could take him -
                but he left his ears behind.

Now our Albert's a celebrity
    and rabbits far and wide,
Come to hear of his adventure,
    when, half eaten he survived.
But Black Tom the scourge of Rabbit Land
    is never far away,
Watching out for Albert,
    to eat the rest of him some day!!

SAMMY AND SUSIE

It was early autumn at the end of the 1990's when the doorbell rang one evening. A gentleman that I vaguely knew lived on the outskirts of the village, stood on the doorstep, clutching a shoebox.

"Do you think you could take in a kitten, I found it wandering round the garden, and I'm allergic." I opened the box, and was greeted by the most ugly kitten I'd ever seen. She was a mere scraggy handful, with a narrow ratty face, huge eyes and hardly any whiskers. (The poor little sod, I thought, nobody else will want this.)

I gave her milk and food which she accepted, sorted her out with a comfy box and a hot-water bottle wrapped in a jumper, and before long she was happily asleep. I had acquired a new kitten, who I christened Susie.

It was twenty four hours later. Susie was settling nicely, and being in equal measure bossed and mothered by the other cats.

The phone rang, it was the gentleman from yesterday. "Have you still got that kitten?"

Well, yes, she was asleep, twitching in her box. "I've got another one," he said, "some tourists have just found an identical kitten wandering down the white line of the main road, crying. It's a miracle it wasn't killed." I told him to send them to me.

They were nice people who'd been staying in a holiday cottage, and were due to go home the next day. They'd been out for an evening walk, when they'd spotted this kitten, and just managed to sweep him up before a car squashed him. It was obvious this was Susie's twin, and if anything he was even uglier!

I brought Susie from the other room, and united the two little scraps. Their noses met, their paws wrapped around each other, and their purrs were lovely to hear. It was a 'God sent' reunion. I hadn't the heart to part them again, so I had two ugly kittens for the price of one!

THE DEAF CAT

She hears no tender words,
bird song is unknown,
alone inside her closed-off life
she wanders mystified,
informed by sight and scent.
She feels my touch,
trusts my hands caressing
her white fur,
but she cannot hear her purr
or high pitched cry.

Sound has no power to stir
her into fear,
near but distant
as she grooms her snowy paws
enclosed in a cocoon
her big moon eyes observe,
they are her windows on the world.

I learn to wake her gently,
skim her fur with whispering breath,
show, not speak my love,
seek her from lost corners
of the house,
become her ears,
her shadow friend.

'GIFTS FOR MUMMY'

My morning gift for Mummy
Was a vole upon the mat,
I proudly sat besides it,
Like a famous hunting cat,
I'd eaten off the back legs
And it's tail was past its best,
But I thought I'd been quite generous
I left her all the rest.

My lunch-time gift for Mummy
Was a dog-eared bit of wren,
I didn't kill it - honest,
And it couldn't fly again.
The feathers nearly choked me,
It was definitely deceased,
I'll never know why Mummy
Said, "I was a horrid beast."

My noon-time gift for Mummy
Was a rabbit minus head,
Well, I had to eat that bit off
To make sure it was dead.
I only nipped in with it
I was sure I'd get it back,
But Mummy put on plastic gloves
And wrapped it in a sack.

My tea-time gift for Mummy
Was a quite large, half-dead rat,
Well, I really tried to kill it
But I'm just a small black cat.
I left it on the staircase,
But it tumbled down a few,
Now Mummy's having brandy,
And I'm hiding in the loo.

After such exhaustions,
It's nearly time for sleep,
But I've one gift left to give her,
That really will not keep.
So I've jumped up on her empty lap
To give a plaintive plea,
That now I've got a tummy ache -
So, I've sicked all down her knee!

MY MOTHER'S CAT

My Mother's cat
> is a grumpy feline,

She looks upon blood
> as a fine vintage wine,

She hates all the neighbours
> and most other cats,

She much prefers fingers
> to field mice or rats,

Her teeth hunt for shin-bones,
> no flesh is immune,

If she misses at breakfast
> she'll have you by noon.

My Mother's cat

        is an awkward feline,

Determined to have her own way

        every time,

Lord Help the human

        who sits in her chair

She'll dig in with her claws

        and shed clouds of hair,

She'll pummel and pound

        as if kneading the dough,

Then take half your skirt

        when she deems to let go.

My Mother's cat

      is a bossy feline,

With one swipe of her paw

      she keeps big cats in line,

That glint in her eye

      means that trouble's to come

Then she'll stalk round the room

      like Atilla The Hun,

No-one would dare cross her

      from a cat to a mouse,

As my Mother's cat

      is the Boss of the house.

PEARLY

To be the friend of a deaf cat, is not easy. Normal words and actions are not appropriate, and can even be the cause of fear. A cat who is deaf cannot be called, does not hear you approach, what she sees and smells is all she knows. A tender touch is welcomed but not without warning, a sudden hand from behind will only startle.

I received an unexpected phone call just before Christmas about twenty years ago. This white cat had been found straying round Penrith, and had been taken to a cattery in Appley. They had tried to find her a home without success, and now with the onset of the festive season, with a fully booked cattery, they had no room for her.

"If you don't have her, she'll have to go to the vet's, to be put to sleep," I was told, "she's such a love, and she only bites a bit!"

Always a soft touch, (and I only had six cats already, all rescued strays,) I told the lady to bring her along.

She arrived some hours later. Pure white, with golden eyes and enormous whiskers. I let her out of the cat basket, and she immediately made herself at home on the couch. The cat in residence on the couch, spat and sissed, but the white cat never batted an eye-lid.

"This is going to be easy," I said, sliding a hand gently down her back. She promptly jumped like she'd been stabbed, spun round and dug her teeth in me.

We had an uneasy day. At times she was gentleness itself, at others she was more like a wild-cat, striking without warming, swift with both teeth and claws.

The cats have their own room, and since it was now five days before Christmas Day, I really didn't have the time to spend with a temperamental feline. Come bedtime I just popped her on the bed in the centre of the cats. They created an awful rumpus, hissing and spitting, the white lady took absolutely no notice. Only when the senior Tom tapped her on the nose did she respond with a swift retaliation, after a short boxing match Tom retired with his pride hurt, and peace resumed.

When I went in the next morning the cats had decided she was very thick-skinned, and that loud protestations of their annoyance brought no response. In disgust they gave up, I think they came to the conclusion 'she was a bit dim'.

It took me a few days to 'cotton-on'. I noticed she never turned to my voice, would sit by the hoover un-stirring, most of the cats were terrified by the noise it made. When I clattered the plates and knocked the tin-opener against a tin of cat food, indicating meal times, she would just carry on with what ever she was doing. But the most noticeable thing was that when I opened up the cats bedroom in the morning where the others would bound out, Pearly that's what I'd christened her, slept on. The first few mornings I just gave her a little tap, and she would shoot up alarmed, disorientated. Then the light dawned - of course, Pearly was deaf.

I now went through a series of tests, clapping hands behind her head, popping a balloon. She never turned her head, no matter what the sound, it was now patently clear, she had no hearing at all.

Once the discovery was made, a whole new way of communicating had to be developed. It was essential to always approach her whenever possible from the front. It was no use calling her, but I had to wave a hand under her nose and indicate what I wanted, or where I wished her to go. I never touched her when she was asleep, but blew across her ears or neck fur. This woke her gently, and she would stretch, roll over, and meow 'hallo'.

Other problems slowly presented, not only was she deaf, but she had no sense of direction, her natural sense of place was missing, and she regularly became lost in the house, especially on the long upstairs corridor. Since she was deaf she couldn't hear herself cry, and her high-pitched wailing easily penetrated the ceiling, and I was always running upstairs to rescue her.

Because of this problem she could never be allowed to go out unsupervised, because she just got lost. I found she had a tendency to walk in a straight line, if that ended at a wall that's where she stopped, and the wailing began. She didn't seem to be able to turn around and retrace her steps.

On one occasion she slipped out and unknown to me headed down the farm yard. In a panic I found she was missing, and the hunt was on. We scoured the house, no sign, so began outside. Just beyond the yard gate some men were working with pneumatic drills digging up the road, the noise was terrible.

I waited until they stopped and asked them if they'd seen a white cat. "Yes, she's been sitting here watching us, never known a cat do that before," said the one. I explained she was deaf. In silence we listened, I knew if she was lost and had met a dead-end she would have stopped.

Then we all heard her, this tremendous wailing, but where was it coming from? I followed the sound, and discovered she'd gone into the neighbours open garage. She'd walked until she'd arrived at the corner, her way blocked she had just sat down crying, waiting to be saved.

I blamed her biting on the deafness. It did get better as she settled, but I could never trust her with strangers. She looked so adorable that everyone wanted to stroke her, only to be greeted with a full set of very sharp teeth! It became habitual to tell people to 'Beware of the white cat'.

She had many strange ways but her most amusing was her ability to steal other cats food. She would gobble her own, she was very greedy, then hook a claw over the rim of someone else's saucer, and before they knew their food was heading off. It was clear Pearly would never starve.

She was also a very motherly cat, who would curl up with any cat who was ill, she would keep an old cat warm, and take any new kitten under her protection.

I grew to love her dearly, and she lived with us for over twelve years, until she succumbed to old age, and passed away as quietly as she had lived.

I would never hesitate to have a deaf cat again, for as I realised Pearly was very special.

CAT WITH A MOUSE

Caught!

Flesh ensnared in practised jaws,

Fur crushed in needle claws,

Terror, bulging eyes of pain

Begging to be free again.

The struggling plaything crawls

across the ground,

Without a sound

The cat springs, hope is trapped,

The toy dead, its backbone snapped!

SNARLING SAM

When dustbin lids are clanging
Tin cans clash about,
Windows rap and rattle
Rain gushes down the spout,
A whisker stirs in warning
As the word spreads up and down,
"Watch out! We're in for trouble
 Snarling Sam's in town."

A desperado of the darkness
Eyes of emerald green
Never miss a movement,
But he passes by unseen,
His razor claws are pointed
His teeth can rip and tear,
He's hated by the other cats
But Snarling Sam don't care.

King of countless conflicts,
Victims stain his path,
He'll leave them torn and bloodied
And pass by with a laugh,
You'll just hear distant crying,
Find a mass of shredded hair
But the battle ground's deserted
Snarling Sam's not there.

He'll hunt them round the houses,
He'll leave no stone unturned,
They can rush indoors for safety
But the fight is just adjourned,
He'll be waiting round the corner
For some unsuspecting paws,
Soon he'll have them at the mercy
Of Snarling Sams' sharp jaws.

He's the cut-throat of the roof-tops,
The terror of the night,
A gangster trimmed with whiskers
Who sets the streets a-fright,
But when he's home from battle
Purring on the mat,
Snarling Sam's an angel,
Just a sweet old pussy-cat.

Sunny

We didn't mean to keep him
But he stayed for twenty years,
All he asked was comfort
He gave us love and purrs.
He never rowed with other cats
That would have been unkind,
And he didn't have a wicked bone
Or a wrong thought in his mind.

He ate what he was given
He never picked or poked,
He never came in dirty
With his coat all ruffed and soaked.
We took him much for granted
And forgot that he was there
Gazing through the window,
Or curled up in a chair.

He liked an evening cuddle
And vibrated all the while,
He had that sort of happy face
That always seemed to smile.
I never saw him angry
Or even twitch his tail,
He had this cheerful personality
That never seemed to fail.

He was the perfect gentleman
Without a single flaw,
His manners were impeccable,
He'd never bite or claw,
That's why we called him Sunny
And he lived up to his name,
And of all the cats that I have loved,
I'll not see his like again.

THE STREAK OF WILD

There's a streak of wild in the cat
on my knee,
When he's out on his travels,
I never will see
Him tearing the mouse
or shredding the bird,
Creeping on paws, that never are heard,
Licking his lips as he straggles his kill,
Ripping warm flesh,
'till he's taken his fill,
Spitting out feathers, flashing a claw,
Tossing his prize with a flick of his paw,
He'll challenge a rival,
arched like the moon
Shrieking displeasure -
and then very soon
He'll be back in the house,
as it's time for his tea
This wide streak of wild,
the cat on my knee.

A DAY IN THE LIFE OF A CAT

My life is very hectic,
I wake at 6am,
Have some morning nibbles,
Then back to sleep again.

I might stir at eleven,
and take a gentle stroll,
Before back into the kitchen,
"Now what is in my bowl?"

I suppose I better have a wash,
I'll do my paws and head,
This cushion's awfully comfy
I'll just go back to bed.

She disturbs me in the afternoon,
her manners are quite poor,
To come and steal my resting place
And put me on the floor!

Since I've been so rudely woken,
I'll need some extra care,
So I'll have to prod upon her knee,
While she strokes my silken hair.

It must be nearly tea-time,
I hope I get to choose
From fishy chunks or jellied beef,
Before my evening snooze.

I stretch about 8.30,
yawn and lick a pad,
Inspect the bed-time menu,
Discover it's not bad.

How dare she keep me waiting,
I've had little food today,
And the few crumbs that I've managed,
Have digested quite away.

At last I've had my supper,
I'm feeling rather worn,
It's been an age since breakfast,
And I've been up since dawn.

This sofa's so relaxing,
I don't want to wash or play,
I'll just settle down and close my eyes,
And dream the night away.

SO MANY CATS

There are so many cats
I remember with love,
who have all flown away
to that cat-cloud above,
they stayed for awhile and
shared in my life,
one saw me grow from
a child to a wife.
Some came as small bundles
of whiskers and fur,
and slept in my arms with
a twitch and a purr,
others arrived bedraggled
and thin,
from a long weary road

and just wandered in.

All were unwanted,

unloved and alone,

searching for comfort,

a meal and a home.

But whatever I gave them

they returned many-fold,

my furry companions

are worth more than gold.

THE CHRISTMAS CAT

The Christmas cat has sent "Good wishes"
For bowls of milk and meat and fishes,
For balls of wool and a nice warm bed,
To the cats round the corner,
Ginger and Fred.

The Christmas cat has bought his presents,
He's sending me a brace of pheasants,
There's sardine for Humphrey
and roast pork for Tim,
On the clear understanding
we share them with him.

The Christmas cat has trimmed his tree,
With glitter, quince and filigree,
With, 'Clever Boy' chocolates
and catnip mice,
And a fluffy-blue rabbit, that looks quite nice.

The Christmas cat has planned his day,
Breakfast in bed on his special tray,
Turkey and goose for lunch-time spread,
Cream for tea, and an early bed.

The Christmas cat is such a size!
From his portly tum to his large gold eyes,
As his New Year diet hovers near,
He wishes Christmas could last all year.

(First printed in 'Footprints in the Snow' poems for Christmas, Jackie Huck, Mill House Originals.)

ALFIE -

'LITTLE FRIEND OF ALL THE WORLD'

Alfie first turned up at the M6 Service Station, just outside the village. Jet black, about four months old, he was discovered wandering around soaked in diesel! Where he had come from no one knew, or how he'd got into this sorry state. Left without help he would have died from trying to wash all the diesel off his fur.

One of the young chaps from the village who was working there, took Alfie into the back of the Services, and soaped and cleaned him. This exceptionally affectionate kitten emerged from the cleaning, and trying to fix him up with a home, it was arranged that a young couple from Orton, who already had three cats would take him in.

Alfie was promptly brought into the village and should have settled down without any further problems, but his new cat family would have none of him. He decided he could do better, so he moved out, and took up residence in the village centre.

Soon everyone was talking about this very friendly kitten, who seemed to be checking everyone out. He seemed to draw up a rota, and in turn followed most people home. On arrival either they didn't want him, or after a quick inspection of the facilities, even though encouraged to stay, Alfie found the new accommodation wanting. I first met him after he'd been wandering around for a couple of weeks. I was delivering the milk when I was accosted by this black kitten, who meowed to introduce himself, was soon purring and demanding a cuddle. We were a big hit, but I already had enough cats, and tried to reserve a place for some poor scrap who no-body else wanted. This cat had about ten homes on offer!

Over the next few weeks we met up regularly near the shop, and I decided to 'lay it on the line'.

"Now see here Alfie, (I called him that from the minute we met, it somehow was perfect) lots of people want to give you a home, but - if you manage to make your

way by yourself to our house, you can stay."
He eyed me with those great golden orbs of
his, purring even harder.

A week passed and I met him again, at the
far end of the village, he was getting further
away not nearer, a good ten minute walk
from here. We had a similar conversation,
and I climbed back in the van, and drove off.

A week later we were coming home from the
early morning milk round, as we rounded
our corner leading to the farm, a small
black cat was waiting. I stopped the van.
"Well, you've about made it. Do you want
to come?" He jumped onto my knee, and
I drove him the last few yards. He walked
into the house, had a meal, and was soon
asleep. It took him just a couple of days to
make friends with the other cats, and only
about five days before I let him out - but I
knew he wasn't going anywhere. Alfie had
made his choice, and found his home.

THE CAT AND THE MOON

There was once a cat

Kind-a round and fat,

With eyes like amber lights,

She'd a constant purr

With silky fur,

She'd creep around at nights,

She'd gaze at the stars

Venus and Mars,

But the one who made her swoon,

Was that golden eye

King of the sky,

The silent Man in the Moon.

The cat would sing

To that shining thing,

'Till the neighbours cursed her song,

But she'd fallen in love

With that Man above,

How could her love be wrong?

So, she packed her gear,

"I'll clear out of here,"

She sang with a lonesome rhyme,

"If I climb up high,

I can touch the sky,

And meet that Man of mine."

She set off down the street

On her four little feet,

'Till she came to the old oak tree,

"If I climb up that

Like a brave little cat,

My Man will smile at me."

So up she climbed,

(Whilst the church clock chimed)

To a hollow far above,

And there she clung,

While her small voice sung

The praises of her love.

Then, out of the air,

Stretched a golden stair,

Which shone with a sparkling light,

And a beckoning hand

From that magic land,

Led her off into the night.

So far away

Where the star-men play,

You can sometimes hear the tune,

The singing cat

Content and fat,

Who loves the Man in the Moon.

CHUMMY

Chummy was a bully! Just like some children, some cats are bullies.

He arrived a small bundle of fluffy tabby, and he grew into a magnificent creature. Extremely beautiful, his fur made him look round, his cheeks stripped out, his neck ruff stood out like a Tudor Queen.

He towered over the other cats, and naturally gravitated to Top Cat. The others understood the pecking order. Chummy had the first bowl of food, Chummy always had the best place on the couch, the comfiest cushion, the centre of the bed. Chummy insisted on the largest amount of attention, and heaven help, the unwise cat who dared to put a paw on 'mothers knee' if Chummy was in residence.

New kittens and cats were rapidly put in their place. A few thumps and they knew better than to argue. Chummy reigned supreme, until one terrible day, when he met his 'Armmagedon'. It was his own fault. A large stray black cat was roaming the territory. He was causing no trouble, and kept well away from the residents. Since all my cats were neutered he had no bone to pick with the toms, and no amorous chances with the She cats. But Chummy couldn't accept this peaceful situation, and went looking for trouble.

I heard the cat-fight, but never saw it. Cat screeches came from somewhere in the undergrowth, but where in the darkness I couldn't tell. A short while later Chummy returned. He was like a half-drowned rat, his beautiful tabby fluff drenched. It looked like he'd been in the stream. On examination amazingly there was not a mark on him. No blood, bites or raggy ears, just wet. A good towelling, and a bowl of warm milk would seem to resolve the problem.

He appeared to have recovered the next morning, but unusual for him would not go out, and instead huddled under the lamp, his head down on his chest, and so it continued.

His appetite, once indecently huge, shrunk to irregular nibbles. His magnificent coat became dull, the weight dropped off him, and now worried, I took him to the vet. He could find nothing wrong. No temperature, no infections, no internal problems, physically Chummy was fine. I explained to the vet about the cat fight, and his behaviour ever since.

"He's suffering from depression," he said to my amazement. "He's always been top cat, now he's been knocked off his throne, and it's made him sulk, and become depressed."

Well, I'd never heard the like, I didn't think cats could become depressed, but it really was the only explanation. I asked the vet what I could do, and he thought it would just take time for Chummy to recover his confidence. "Give him lots of love and attention," he said, "and he should come round."

It took nearly a year. I spoiled him rotten, lots of cuddles and admiration. Special treats to eat, toys, time put aside to play with him. Telling him how lovely he was, (I'm sure he understood) and letting him sit on my knee whenever I had the time. Slowly his appetite picked up, and he reluctantly moved away from the lamp where he'd taken refuge.

It took six months for him to build up his confidence to go outside again, by this time thankfully, the rogue tom cat had moved on. I think on the quiet, the others were a bit smug that Chummy had 'got what was coming to him', and I don't think they gave him any sympathy, but they were respectful enough not to take advantage of his 'fall', and though he never bullied them again, he was still the Top Cat.

THE OLD CAT

I'm an old grey cat letting life slip by,
Nothing disturbs as I twitch and sigh,
My silken fur is grizzled and dank,
My sturdy frame is frail and lank.
It's a shadow world as my eye sight dims,
A bony old cat with creaking limbs,
But my heart beats strong with a
faithful thud,
And I have to say, that life's been good.

I've lain for hours in the kindly sun,
Chased autumn leaves just for fun,
I used to climb in the highest tree,
I caught a rat, bigger than me,
I've hunted mice beneath the moon,
Crooned to clouds my special tune,
I've been loved and pampered
and understood,
There's not long left, but it's all been good.

No rain-soaked nights with dripping hair
But a warm fireside and my favourite chair,
No fight for life in a friendless world,
Just contented dreams on a cushion curled.
No harsh words on a lonely street,
But a gentle voice and the best to eat,
No hungry stray round the
neighbour-hood,
Yes, I've been lucky, and life's been good.

My hours pass slowly, I sleep all day,
But I sometimes watch while the young
ones play
Remembering times when I rushed around,
With agile paws that made no sound.
Then a tender hand strokes my ragged fur,
And I fall asleep with a peaceful purr,
As I drift serenely towards the end,
I know I've lived with a cats best friend.

LEARNING TO SAY

GOODBYE

You won't be long old man,

I know you have to go

It must be so.

I try to prepare my mind,

For when you've gone

And I am left behind,

For I was blessed

The day you strayed

My way, and stayed.

For Monty. R.I.P.

About the Poet

Jackie Huck was born in Liverpool, but grew up on Ashton-under-Lyne, Lancashire, in the 1950's against the background of the fading cotton industry. She lived in a tiny house pushed between warehouses and shop backs, with no neighbours or playmates.

An only child: from an early age cats became her friends and companions. Many were kittens rescued from the streets or sad waifs who strayed into the yard. This was the basis for a life-long 'love affair' with a string of feline friends.

She moved to Cumbria in 1974 working as a District Nurse, before marrying a local farmer in 1976 and settling down to nurse cows and cats.

She has written poetry from childhood, much of it reflecting the Industrial North of her childhood, the beauty of her adopted Cumbria, and of course her cats.